I0533291

A Journey Through Grief

Annie Brown

A Journey Through Grief

Annie Brown

2024 © by Annie Brown

All rights reserved. Published 2024.

No part of this publication may be reproduced or transmitted in any form or by any means, electronic or mechanical, including photocopying, recording, or any information storage and retrieval system now known or yet to be invented, without written permission from the publisher, except in cases of brief quotations in critical articles and reviews.

Printed in the United States of America

Spirit Media and our logos are trademarks of Spirit Media

SpiritMedia.US

www.spiritmedia.us

8045 Arco Corporate Dr STE 130

Raleigh, NC 27617

1 (888) 800-3744

Kindle Store › Kindle eBooks › Self-Help

Paperback ISBN:
Library of Congress Control Number:

Introduction

I have been involved in grief counseling/ministry for over 15 years now, but acquainted with grief in a very intimate way for almost 34 years. It was not the ministry that I would have chosen for myself, given the choice. I was an excellent Sunday School teacher, sang in the choir, and taught Bible studies. I felt like my life was full of ministry, but I didn't know then that there were other plans for my future.

What I know now is that, out of my loss, out of the deepest darkest season of my life, my ministry was born.

The pain of loss feels almost unbearable, and absolutely nothing makes sense. I remember after my husband was killed just 2 weeks after his 36th birthday, my 16-year-old son and I went to live with my mother. I had no idea how to care for the livestock or manage our home, including a wood burner we relied on for heat. At the time, we had an outdoor dog that I fed using a glass plate. It had been several days since I had been at the house, and the grass desperately needed cutting. As I approached the front steps, I stepped on the glass plate hidden in the overgrown grass, and It broke into several pieces. Even after all these years, I remember looking down at the broken plate and saying aloud, "You might as well break….everything else in my life is broken."

Out of my sorrow, I learned how to connect with hurting people, how to minister to them, help them, and show them that although they cannot believe it now, in the middle of their darkest season, there IS life after death.

A quick overview of how I became acquainted with grief is this. When I was in my mid-30s, my husband was killed when the piece of machinery he was driving overturned. I was left with broken dreams and a 16-year-old son. Ten weeks later, Dave's wife was killed in a car accident, leaving him with a 17-year-old daughter and a 15-year-old son.

Dave and I knew each other from the church we attended although our families never socialized. The following year, we got married. Together we became a grieving couple, with three grieving kids. Needless to say, life was interesting. Only **sometimes** easy, but interesting nonetheless.

Over the next few years, we learned an important truth: There is life after death. And that life can be filled with unimaginable joy and happiness. Does it happen overnight? No, and I must add, it is intentional to get back into living life to the fullest.

But be assured, **THERE IS LIFE AFTER DEATH, I AM LIVING PROOF.**

Key Takeaways

The first lesson will be the longest and probably the most in-depth. I will often cite my personal experiences because, of course, that is what I know best. These lessons will be an introduction to what grief can look like, the most important word here is CAN. People are often unaware of the emotions that can accompany the loss of a loved one.

I often tell people in our groups that describing what grief can look and feel like is a bit like trying to tell someone what a chocolate milkshake is like if they have never in their life experienced one. First, it's cold and thick but can become not quite as cold and it will get thinner if it's not consumed quickly. It tastes chocolatey, but not like a chocolate candy bar-it is sweet and it is smooth, but depending on the ingredients, it could be sort of chunky, and it can take on other tastes if they add coffee or nuts or any number of additional ingredients to make it individual. Here's a big thing, if you take too big of a drink of it, you can get a thing called "Brain Freeze"....doesn't that sound like something everyone should want to try?

Please be aware that all grief does not look alike, there is no "How To" manual. Grief is very individual.

LESSON 1

Living with grief

LET'S TAKE A LOOK

HELP!!!! What just happened to me?????

Is he really not coming home?

I thought I heard her car!!

I just want to talk to my best friend one more time!

It's not fair!!!

I need my mom, dad, son, daughter, sister, brother, grandparent!

This CAN'T be the way it is!!!

I JUST WANT MY LIFE BACK!

When someone close to us dies, it seems like our world spins out of control because of three things:

1. NOTHING IS AS VAST AS THE VALLEY OF GRIEF.
2. NOTHING IS AS BIG AS LOSING OUR "EVERY DAY', OUR "NORMAL."
3. NOTHING IS AS LIFE-CHANGING AS KNOWING OUR LOVED ONE HAS TAKEN THEIR LAST BREATH HERE ON EARTH.

Depending on who the person was that died (spouse, father, mother, sibling, or whoever it is that we loved), along with the pain of the actual physical "miss", we experience the loss of so many other things called "secondary losses."

*Companionship

*That every night phone call

*Family connection

*Income/Health Insurance

*A house full of laughter

*The cook, shopper, mechanic, bill payer, the mower

*The loss of our dreams: retirement, the kids growing up, getting married and having grandkids

*A host of other losses that only YOU can know.

Often, the pain of loss can be overwhelming.

When it rocks YOUR world, you think you will never get better. Every day is filled with darkness and every day is filled with pain and heaviness. There is overwhelming sadness that feels endless. And please remember, there is nothing wrong with grieving, it's not a sign of weakness and it does not mean you don't trust God.

When a loved one receives a terminal diagnosis, grief often begins before death. The knowledge that time is limited brings a sense of urgency, and though hope remains, fear accompanies it. Similarly, when death follows a long illness or old age, you may feel somewhat prepared, but the emptiness that follows is unexpected. Whether anticipated or sudden, the pain of loss is profound, leaving us questioning if we could have done something differently.

When tragedy strikes unexpectedly—whether it's a sudden accident or a suicide—there are no last goodbyes, no words of reconciliation, and no chance for closure. The pain is accompanied by haunting questions: Could I have helped? Why didn't I see the signs? These questions linger long after the shock fades. But in time, you realize that some griefs don't need answers. Healing comes not from understanding, but from learning to live with the loss.

Suicide brings its own unique pain, filled with guilt and confusion. My son struggled with the guilt of not answering his friend's call on the day he died. We all wonder, "Could I have prevented this?" But no matter how much we wish we could change the past, we can't. Healing comes not from answering these questions but from honoring their memory, accepting the pain, and learning to move forward.

Death forever changes the contours of our lives, but I can tell you as a living testament, that recovering from the death of a loved one IS possible. I am not the same person I was when my husband was killed 33 years ago. Had I not gone through that life-changing experience, I would not be the person that I am today.

GRIEF IS A NATURAL RESPONSE TO LOSS

"Grief is the price you pay for loving someone--if there were no love, there would be no grief." This quote by Zig Ziglar truly reflects why we feel such pain when we lose a loved one. We feel pain because there was love.

We don't grieve when the Mailman's uncle's best friend from when he was a kid dies. Grief is reserved for those that we have loved.

Life becomes so intense due to grief. Sometimes you think you are never going to get better.

Not only is grief hugely mentally distractive, but it can disrupt your physical health as well. Grieving can make it difficult to sleep, or you want to sleep all the time. It can be hugely disorienting. Gaining or losing weight is normal.

A program called "GriefShare" talks about the emotions we can feel after death as a "Tangled Ball of Emotions." These emotions can include pain, rage, anxiety, abandonment, anger, envy, loneliness, dread, depression, bitterness, confusion, fear, resentment, sorrow, dismay, apathy, guilt, shock, disbelief, and numbness.

There never seems to be just ONE emotion. In a day you can feel any number of emotions. Sometimes when all of these emotions are rolling around in our head, that's when people feel like God has left them. At times like that, we are just being human. God has not gone anywhere. He is right where He has always been–beside us. Remember what He has said in His Word in Deuteronomy 31:8, "And the

Lord, He it is that doth go before thee; He will be with thee, He will not fail thee, neither forsake thee: fear not, neither be dismayed."

It's also when all these emotions are flying around in us, that we start with the questions that don't seem to stop.

Why and What if?

Pondering questions without answers is like a hamster on a wheel. The questions can roll around and around and around in your head. There just aren't any answers to all the "what if's" or "why's". What if I had only said? What if I hadn't said? If I would have only... What if I hadn't done it? What if I had paid closer attention to the symptoms? What if I hadn't let them take the car that night? He was struggling, why didn't I see that? Why didn't she tell me about the lump?

There just are no answers to why we face losses, but we can rest in the promise that He will never leave us.

Grief recovery is a process.

Psalms 23 reminds us that "Yea, though I walk **THROUGH** the valley of the shadow of death..." It is something that we get through. A Journey Through Grief IS an apt description.

Personally, in my valley of grief, I distinctly remember thinking "I cannot live the rest of my life feeling like this. I just can't." I had to believe that I was going to get better. We must believe that we will get **THROUGH** the grieving process, **THROUGH** the pain.

Working through grief may seem like navigating a long dark tunnel. After my husband was killed, I truly felt like I was in a long dark tunnel that I could not see my way out of. It felt like the longer I went, it just did not get any better. I can say standing on this side of the valley, there is light at the end of the tunnel.

Anyone who has experienced the death of a loved one has probably been told at some point, 'Grief is temporary.' Amid grief, it's almost impossible to believe things will get better. No one can convince you otherwise, and hearing those words can even provoke anger.

Sometimes, all we think Is "I just want to shut off the pain." That can be done with alcohol, drugs (prescription or illegal), shopping, overeating, sleeping, and any number of things.

These fixes are only temporary.

It is unhealthy to numb the pain. It does not solve anything, but rather prolongs the grieving process and just piles on additional problems.

Often, people feel like they just don't want to live. They feel like they have nothing to live for now that their loved one is gone.

People say they hate life. It's not that they hate life, it's that they hate life the way it is right now, filled with pain and hurt.

Remember, **IT IS NOT TRUE THAT THE WAY YOU THINK AND FEEL NOW IS THE WAY YOU WILL ALWAYS THINK AND FEEL.**

Even though you cannot believe that you will EVER feel right again, you will.

Recovering from the loss we have experienced IS possible, but it is not like waking up after having a bout with the flu. We are not grieving one day and "back to normal" the next day. You cannot think it away, you cannot wish it away, and you cannot ignore it away. Grief recovery just does not work like that. Grief recovery is intentional and it takes work.

One of the biggest things to help move you forward is to believe you are going to get better. On this journey through the valley of grief, there will be good days, and there will be bad days, and truly, at first, the bad days outnumber the good. Just hold on, better days are on the horizon.

Key Takeaways

There is nothing wrong with grieving.

Grief really is the price you pay for loving someone

Grief is temporary, even though you don't believe it right now.

It is not healing to medicate with alcohol, drugs, etc. It just prolongs the hurting.

We are not used to processing so many emotions at once.

Life becomes so intense and grief is mentally disruptive during the grieving process

Grief recovery is not like waking up after a bout with the flu, IT IS A PROCESS.

IT IS NOT TRUE THAT THE WAY I THINK AND FEEL NOW IS THE WAY I AM ALWAYS GOING TO THINK AND FEEL.

You must believe that you will make it. Life WILL get better.

LESSON 2

How do I live with this life changing event?

Is what I am feeling normal, or am I losing my mind?

*My pain is so intense I feel like I am dying!

*How do I go on when all I want to do is curl up and die too?

*All I do is cry!

*No one understands why I don't return phone calls, go shopping, hang out with friends anymore, and do nursery duties now. They just don't get it!

*I can't remember what her voice sounded like.

*I am afraid of forgetting him.

*I JUST WANT MY LIFE BACK THE WAY IT WAS!

As stated in Lesson One, all these feelings are normal, and to be truthful, if you have experienced a significant loss (not the cat, not great, great uncle Herman, or the neighbor's mother's friend that lived in Australia), but a true, close personal loss, you may have felt any or all of those things.

We have also said that grief is reserved for those that we have loved. **The closer the loss is to us, the more intense the grief will be.**

It's OK to not be OK.

After the death of a loved one, it is normal to feel sad, upset or lost. Don't be angry with yourself for feeling sad.

Don't try to cover it by saying to yourself, "Man up" "Get a grip" or even saying "Just get over it".

If someone wants you to "snap out of it", they more than likely have never been through the loss of someone close to them. There is no "snapping out of it" because remember, grief is a process.

There is no right way or wrong way to grieve. Grief is highly individual. There are no books or roadmaps to tell us how to do it "right" or "The 5 best ways to grieve." There are no "How-to" videos when it comes to grief, and even though you can search on YouTube "How to shoot a grizzly bear" and "How to get rid of gnats", you can't search on Google or YouTube ***"The Ten Best Ways to Stop the Pain When Someone You Love Dies."*** You can find many sites that talk about the grieving process and the journey you are now in, but there is no quick fix to grieving.

There is no schedule to stick to, and there is no timeframe.

Our society (including our jobs) only gives us three days of bereavement to plan and have a funeral. We can't process much in three days. People are often forced back to work before any of the legal things are settled. I had to return to work because we had bills to pay, and I had to pick up the insurance. And most of the time, FMLA (Family Medical Leave Act) does not cover bereavement time.

In reality, it takes up to two years to fully process the loss of your loved one. Just because it has been a month, many months, a year, or several years, it doesn't mean it is the end of grief.

Everyone's grief is unique.

This journey is so individual. That cannot be stressed enough. When we say there is no right or wrong way to grieve, it is because we are individuals and what I might find relief in, another might find it only brings greater pain. When people are grieving a fresh loss, there are a lot of things we do either consciously or unconsciously as we muddle along. Again, please excuse the personal reference, my story is what I know best. I found comfort in sleeping with my husband's blue jeans. When I went to stay at my mom's, I brought five pairs of them with me. She could tell what kind of day I had experienced by how many pairs of his pants I had tucked around me at night when I went to bed. If I had a good day there was only a pair or two, if it was one of "those" days, then all five pairs would be tucked around me. I did talk to my doctor about it. Actually, he was the coroner at the time of Ron's death and knew the specifics of my situation intimately. I told him I could smell him when I had his jeans beside me. He did assure me that I wasn't losing my marbles, that his scent would fade over time, and by then, I probably wouldn't feel the need for his clothing around me. And you know, he was right.

How you grieve really depends on many factors, including your: **personality, coping style, life experiences, and faith.**

So I guess I am saying it's OK to take comfort in different measures (routines that you might have had, continuing to celebrate birthdays or anniversaries, things that bring you comfort). Just remember, alcohol, drugs, and even prescription meds only compound and prolong the process.

Because the absence of my loved one will change my life, at first every thought can be painful.

For months, I felt my loss so deeply, that I couldn't think of Ron without hurt and pain. I couldn't remember the love, laughter, and good times we shared through the 18+ years of marriage. All of my thoughts were centered on my loss of him. It did take time and effort on my part to bring my thoughts of the good times to the front and let them be the overriding driver of my feelings.

Grief is a process or a journey

This has been stated repeatedly in this book. And that has been intentional. No one is born walking. It is something that we learn as we grow. The same thought is applied to grief. We learn as we go through it, and as it was stated before, this journey of grief doesn't come with a manual.

Time does NOT heal, but it is a great buffer.

Time does not heal all wounds, but what time does however, is teach us how to live with the pain while we are in the healing process.

Possibly, the hurt feels so fresh, or so new, that you can't see that life will get better for you, and I have stood where you are now, not just thinking about it, but saying out loud, "It's never going to get better, it's never going to end, this hurt is never going to heal." But I can tell you, it will. **IF YOU ALLOW** the grieving process to take place, you will make it through this time of pain and hurt.

Tears are very therapeutic.

I often tell the people who attend our grief classes, "I am not afraid of your tears." I don't say that because I am hardened to people's feelings, I just want them to know it's ok to cry. I say it because I understand the value of emptying up bottled feelings.

I remember my current husband, Dave, telling me that after his first wife, Diane, was killed in a car accident, he just laid on their bed and wailed. It was his way of releasing all the pent-up feelings and emotions.

Tears are not a sign of weakness, and please don't think I'm being sexist, but often, men have a harder time crying out their pain than women. Many times those who bottle up their emotions develop physical ailments that have no explanations as well as emotional problems (anger, no longer feeling joy).

Finally for this lesson–.

Faith does not isolate us from tragedy.

What faith does, is sustain us **through** our loss.

Remember this, "When the dust of my sorrow settles, God is standing there next to me. HE has dust on His shoulders as well, because HE has been there all along."

The sovereignty (supreme power or authority) of God can be hard to accept, but it is ultimately a comforting truth to embrace. It is what you can hold on to when you don't understand.

Key Takeaways

How do I deal with this life-changing event?

I really am not losing my mind...

The closer the loss is, the more intense the grief will be.

There is no right way or wrong way to grieve.

There is no schedule to stick to, there is no timeframe.

In reality, it takes up to two years to fully process the loss of a loved one. Everyone's grief is unique.

Someone else's journey should not be the roadmap for our journey.

Because the absence of my loved one forever changes the contours of my life, at first, every thought can be painful.

Grief is a process, a journey.

Tears are very therapeutic.

TIME IS NOT A HEALER, BUT IT IS A GREAT BUFFER.

LESSON 3

Emotions connected with death

I have worked with countless groups of people during their grieving journey. Someone said to me recently, "You never addressed guilt." I am so glad they said that–it was not intentional, so in this lesson, we will talk about a few unique situations that affect our grief. We will also address some practical things in our journey towards healing.

At the end of this lesson, I will include a section called "What I Learned While in my Darkest Hour. Lessons From a Grieving Heart". These remarks are in response to a survey I did with people that have gone through loss.

Let's talk for a minute about an anticipated death.

When someone you love gets a terminal diagnosis, often grieving begins on the day of diagnosis for those connected to them. You begin to realize time is limited and some of your dreams for the future begin to disappear. And although hope is always intermingled with any type of diagnosis, when there has been a terminal diagnosis, fear accompanies that hope.

When death comes after a lengthy illness or even old age, you may think you are prepared, but the reality is, that nothing can prepare you for the loneliness, the emptiness, and the pain that follows the death of a loved one.

When death is an **unexpected tragedy**, there is no way that you can be prepared. A tragic death is accompanied by a different type of grief. There are no last goodbyes, no words of reconciliation or forgiveness, no loving hugs...so much left unsaid.

Sometimes, you just kiss him goodbye in the morning, and he never comes home from work. You tell the kids to drive safely to the ballgame, and the next thing you know, a policeman is at your door. You turn your head for a moment to speak to your friend, and the next minute your toddler is lifeless in the pool.

And then there is the terrible grief that accompanies suicide. When a death occurs from **suicide**, there is often frustration, pain, and questions. Oh, so many questions. The biggest one is WHY?

In addition to dealing with all the emotions that accompany death, now you must also deal with the fact that the person hurt so badly inside that they could actually hurt themselves.

When my son was young, late teens or early 20's, one of his closest friends committed suicide. For a good while, Ronnie struggled with the fact that his friend had called him that day but he did not answer the phone. Would the outcome have been different? Could I have helped him? Haunting questions that have no answers.

You want an answer to WHY?, but often there just is none and the only person that could supply that answer is gone.

When the death is by **murder**, how can you handle that news?

When your loved one has met their death by murder, you can be overloaded with feelings of what occurred.

Did they suffer? Was the murderer caught?

Often, there can be frustration with the judicial system as you wait for some type of justice. Delayed trials are not uncommon but add stress to your already overloaded system.

When a murder has occurred, sometimes you have to deal with anger, bitterness, and resentment. It is important to make sure that you get good Godly counseling when these feelings rise.

When a loss occurs from something that is an **accidental death**, there are also questions of How? Why? Often, the first response is disbelief, followed by the questions.

When Ron was killed, although of course it was an accident, I just wanted to strike out and blame someone. And though there was no one to actually blame, the only one I could find fault with was him. I couldn't figure out why he couldn't just push that machine off himself. He was so big and so strong. That's how skewed our thinking can be under the stress of losing a loved one. When the accidental death is at the hands of someone else (a car accident for example) we MUST make the decision not to be in a constant state of anger or let bitterness hijack our emotions.

It was once said, "**Guilt** is perhaps the most painful companion to death." While I don't completely agree with that statement, guilt **IS** a very painful companion to death.

Guilt can be a common, yet very complex emotion in the grieving process. A person might feel relieved that their loved one is no longer suffering, then feel guilty about the feeling of relief. Someone might feel anger about the circumstances related to the death, and then feel guilty about the feeling of anger.

Guilt is what brings the feelings of "It's my fault," "If only," "I should have," and "I could have done better." There are tons of "Shoulda, Woulda, Coulda" that hold hands with guilt.

(Remember what we learned about the hamster in Lesson 1)

Guilt does not always have to be rational to be real, it is a different kind of beast altogether. It can chase you like a hound dog.

Guilt is a powerful emotion. It can isolate us from others, and alter the way we look at things around us. Guilt causes us to punish ourselves and it very much keeps us focused on our past.

I remember when my husband's mother passed away from cancer in 1998. I will never forget his father's words to me as we were exiting the hospital after she passed. "I will lay her beside my mistake." The reason for those words would break your heart. Almost 35 years before that, his 5-year-old son was on a dozer he was operating when he slipped off and was run over. His father lived almost 10 years after his wife's death, still carrying guilt.

There is such a thing as "false guilt" (my kidney was not a match, I wanted to, but I couldn't help save them. I should have not let her drive in the snow that night, etc.)

We just need to remember that we did the best we could at the time.

Grieving in **conflicted relationships** is a unique aspect of grief.

Because your loved one is gone, don't look for or expect something you can never get. That includes asking forgiveness from the one who is gone, or by telling them in person you forgive them for something they have done, resolution of an argument, or misunderstanding, apologies **to** them, or expressions of regret.

Forgiveness is always a part of the grieving process. But we need to understand that forgiveness is healing for US, not for the other person.

We often have to give forgiveness even if the offender does not deserve it.

Forgiveness sets us free.

A FEW PRACTICAL THINGS:

1. **Often, people ask about items that belong to their loved ones. How long do they keep them, and then what do they do with them?**

    Those decisions are absolutely personal.

    People in my experience have run the gamut, from putting every single thing related to their loved one away to keeping every item of clothing for more than four years.

    Again, those things are individual decisions that should not be allowed to be made by other individuals.

2. **Accept some loneliness.**

    It is completely normal. But at the same time, it is important not to allow yourself to get completely isolated.

3. **Choose good company.**

    Stay in contact with people you are comfortable with. These people won't place any further burdens or expectations on you.

4. **Be gentle with yourself.**

   Try not to judge yourself for not doing better. Remember it's a process.

5. **Get extra rest, but set a regular sleep schedule.**

   Physical and emotional exhaustion is common. You will need more rest than normal.

   Give yourself a good amount of time to rest but be on guard not to sleep too much as a way to avoid the hard work of grieving.

6. **Move your body.**

   Get up and walk or move around at least a little each day. Do not just sit around and dwell on your misery.

7. **Talk to your doctor.**

   It is good for you to keep your doctor informed on what has happened in your life. He or she can help you keep an eye on healthy as well as unhealthy habits.

8. **Keep structure in your day.**

   Bathing and dressing every day even if you are not leaving the house are important to your mental well-being. Eat small regular meals even if you are not hungry.

9. **Be cautious.**

   Don't make knee-jerk decisions.

   Do not make any major decisions or changes in your home or work while in the middle of your grieving.

   Often, death demands decisions (you have to sell the house or it will be foreclosed on, and you need to move back into your parents, siblings, or friends home because now you have no income). Seek qualified help for direction before you make any decisions that will add any additional changes in your already upside-down world.

10. **Don't ignore the need for spiritual strength.**

   Always remember God is an ever-present help in times of trouble.

Key Takeaways

What follows is a compilation of lessons from people who have experienced the death of a loved one and what they learned on their journey.

When people just couldn't understand what I was going through, I learned...**To those that know the pain of it, no explanation is necessary, to those that do not, no explanation is possible.**

I took comfort in knowing that God knows our every thought and emotion...I allowed Him to be my comforter.

One of the best pieces of advice that I got was not AFTER my dad died. It was actually on the day or two after he had been diagnosed with stage four cancer. All I kept saying was "Why? Why my dad?" My dad was a good man, he was a preacher, and he lived what he preached. I just could not figure out why it had to be MY dad. My pastor's wife stopped me and said "Do not try to figure it out. Do not try to figure out why it's YOUR dad. You will never figure it out and you will drive yourself insane trying to figure out why. She told me what I already knew–I had to trust in God, lean on Him, know and understand that God has a perfect plan and while we may not understand it, "all things work for good to those that love Him."

It gets better. It may not seem like it will, but it does get better.

Despite everything you might read or what others might tell you, you never understand it until you experience it yourself.

Grief is very individual. What you experience may not be what someone else experiences. There's no right way or wrong way to deal with grief.

Don't make any big decisions for a year. This was a piece of advice I got and it was right on. You are numb and not thinking straight, so this was huge for us. It was very smart. It takes time and that's OK.

It's OK to talk about them. This has been a huge thing for my family. The kids all loved my dad so much, so they loved to talk about him. We have great memories and love to talk and laugh about the things he did.

Someone told me that grief ebbs and flows and that has always stayed with me. There are definitely triggers, for instance, my dad's birthday and my birthday are very hard for me. My husband misses my father at Christmas.

One of the biggest things for me was to realize that although people will say absolutely the worst things to you, they really do mean well. They just don't know what to say, so a lot of times it ends up coming out wrong. Just let go of that, and don't hold it against them.

Don't try to replace your grief and loneliness with THINGS (shopping was a big one for me). It will just backfire on you and cost you a lot of money.

Give yourself time to grieve. Don't try to rush through the process.

We lost our baby before birth. We bought a rosebush with a plaque in memory of our child. Seeing the roses bloom gave us hope.

Some days, I thought there was something wrong with me because I was so at peace with my son's passing. And then almost right on top of that thought, it would be like I was smacked in the face with the fact that he wasn't just away, he was DEAD!

I've often wondered if it's appropriate to speak about someone after they've passed. For me, the answer is yes. He lived, and I want him to be remembered for the good he brought into the world.

Many thanks to all the people who answered my questions about the things they learned on their journey.

How life will change when your spouse dies

Losing a spouse is a very different kind of loss.

After the death of his wife, a man said to me "I had all this love inside with no place for it to go."

Because of the intimate relationship between a husband and wife, we often feel so "alone." And because of this unique bond, many people around us cannot understand the tremendous loss that a person feels when that bond is broken by death.

You often feel like you have lost your whole life, and in many ways, your life as you knew it before your spouse died is certainly gone. The future as you dreamed it would be including your children growing up with both parents is gone. Thoughts at this time in your life might include:

I don't want to go on... I am so angry at him, I cannot do all of this alone! How will I take care of the kids without her? Cut the grass?? I can't even start the mower! She always did the laundry, how do I start the washer? The car won't start. Who do I call now?? How do I pay the bills without his income? And losses that only you can know.

These are all legitimate questions, and often we don't know or like the answers! Even though we never had to do it before, we often have to learn to accept help from others now. This is especially hard for those who have always leaned on a spouse to take care of household chores or outside work that now must be done by the spouse that is left. When our spouse is gone, we must learn how to manage daily chores because we lean on them for so many things that are really not revealed until they are gone. Our lives certainly become more complex without our spouse, often doubling the workload without any of the pleasures.

After losing a spouse, it can feel like loneliness is your only companion.

As a "single" you now face doing many things alone- eating, sleeping, shopping, and attending church. So many things you did as a couple, must now be done alone. Your friends may seemingly take a step back. Not purposely, but many times friendships revolve around married couples. When your spouse dies, you may feel like a third wheel. It just doesn't feel the same as it did when you were "complete couples."

Again it must be said, that things will never be normal for you again if by "normal" you mean having your spouse back with you, and having what you have lost. **I had to learn that I COULD exist without my husband.** I did not want to, but, I HAD to.

There are many "firsts" without them that we must face when our spouse dies. Some of these things will be:

Your anniversary, birthdays, holidays, the anniversary of their death, and so often, things that only you as a couple celebrated.

Even the small things like eating alone for the first time after they are gone, sleeping alone, dining out alone, attending school functions for the kids, and going to church for the first time without them.

There is often fear of the future.

When my husband was killed, I often drove home listening to a song with the lyrics, "...so this is how without you goes..." I couldn't comprehend that he was truly gone or imagine how I would face the future without him.

One of the big things for me was trying to figure out what I was going to do without his income, without the health insurance that his job provided, and how to manage the small life insurance policy that we had for him.

When our spouse dies, our lives can become so much more complex.

Sometimes if you happen to be a stay-at-home mom, you must find employment.

Sometimes we have had to become entirely responsible for the future of our children. "What would he think we should do?" "How would she handle this situation?

These are times when you ask people in your life for guidance. It is nothing to be ashamed of. Ask your son's best friend›s mom what day is "buy your lunch" day. Ask your sister, mom, or aunt how to do your daughter›s favorite hairstyle, and if you can't manage braids, find a friend who can.

Be careful not to alienate friends when you are grieving.

Grief is very "self-focused" in the beginning. There is nothing wrong with crying, revisiting times spent with your spouse, and "feeling sorry" for yourself to a degree, but there is a time to "broaden" your life again to include others. There is a time when joy will once again become part of your life.

It is possible that you could have thoughts of jealousy or anger towards friends who complain about things that annoy them that their spouse does or does not do. All the time you are thinking "If I just had mine back."

Be careful not to make those around you walk on eggshells trying to avoid upsetting you.

There will be a time when you must intentionally move forward. We move through grief at a different rate than our friends because we live with our grief 24 hours a day, 7 days a week. Our friends go back to their lives. I remember hearing about a woman whose sister just wanted her to go back to being the fun-loving sister that she used to be. She loved going out with her, shopping together, and having fun, but she did not understand that while she would return to her intact family to talk about their day at work and school, her sister would have to go home to an empty house. That same sister came back years later after losing her husband and said to her **"I am so sorry...I did not understand...I do now, I do now."**

It takes time to adjust to this new life we are thrust into.

Be patient with yourself, it takes time.

You won't always get it right, but keep trying.

There may be a time when you have healed and you are ready to move forward with another relationship. There are a few things to remember: Be careful about becoming emotionally involved with someone too soon after the loss of your spouse.

Sometimes the pain feels so great, you just want to shut it off, and often you just want to fill the space with something or SOMEONE.

Be careful not to make any hasty decisions. Judgment is often not good for the first year or so.

You can become emotionally entangled with someone without really being aware that it is happening.

Get good Godly counseling before entering into a relationship after the loss of a spouse. Many times second marriages fail.

Key Takeaways

Losing a spouse is a very different kind of loss.

Because of the intimate relationship between a husband and wife, we often feel so "alone" after the loss of our spouse.

You often feel like you have lost your whole life.

There are so many things you do as a "single" now.

There are many "firsts" without them that we must face when our spouse dies. There is often fear of the future.

When our spouse dies, our lives can become so much more complex. Don't be afraid to ask people in your life for help or guidance. There will be a time when you must intentionally move forward. It takes time to adjust to this new life we are thrust into.

There may be a time when you have healed and you are ready to move forward with another relationship.

Be careful not to make any hasty decisions.

Get good Godly counseling before entering into a relationship after the loss of a spouse.

LESSON 5

Learning to live as a grieving family

One of the things we need to learn, no, we MUST learn, is how to survive and even thrive when a family is dealing with grief.

The loss may be of a mother, father, sibling, or even a beloved grandparent. Whatever the familial loss, it must be acknowledged and care taken to guide the family back to healing.

How to help grieving children.

When a parent dies, the cohesiveness of the family is in danger of being lost. Each member of the family, although feeling loss, can feel it differently. A daughter can feel the loss of her friend, her nurturer, and her shopping buddy. A son can feel the loss of his protector, his mentor, and his guide.

Remember when a child loses a parent or sibling, they grieve differently than adults. They move in and out of grief. One minute they are playing basketball with their buddies, the next, they are in their room sitting in the dark. They do not attend to the loss like adults do. Often they just simply cannot grasp the reality that their parent is no longer able to be with them.

When a sibling dies, the other child (children), not realizing what is happening, can often feel left out of the grieving process. They also can become "jealous" of the attention that their brother or sister is getting from their parents. All they hear is "Johnny loved this", or "Susan was the best kid ever" not understanding that parents often work their way through grief by talking about the child that died.

Kids can express anger toward the remaining parent when one parent dies. They do this in part because there is no way to express their hurt, so they can act inappropriately. LOVINGLY address defiant behavior.

Children will revisit grief at certain milestones; graduation, their wedding, and the births of their own children. They tend to grieve incrementally.

Grief and your family.

When there is a spousal death, remember that your family needs you. It seems like when a husband or wife dies, we forget that the loss reaches beyond the surviving spouse. When there are children, they feel the loss as well. Years after the death of my husband, my son and I were talking. He gently told me, "Mom, after Dad died, I felt like you abandoned me." Believe me, there was nothing that cut so deep as hearing that from my now-grown son. Many years later, I still remember those words.

Be sensitive to your family's needs. Be aware that you are not the only one hurting.

Your child experienced a huge loss too.

To grieve as a healthy family:

- Make sure that you do not do all your grieving behind closed doors in secret.

- It's appropriate for your children to see you sad.

- In a healthy, healing family you must grieve openly because children learn from your behavior.

- Look out for each other.

- Don't blame each other.

- Encourage others to grieve in their own way, at their own pace. Accept new roles in the family.

- Waves of grief can weaken the health of your family. Make sure everyone is getting proper rest and eating adequately.

- Make sure everyone knows it is ok, to talk about the loss the family suffered. It's ok to talk about the one that died. It will help the remaining family unit to heal.

Key Takeaways

We MUST learn how to survive and even thrive when a family is dealing with grief.

Remember when a child loses a parent or sibling, they grieve differently than adults.

Children move in and out of grief.

Kids can express anger toward the remaining parent when one parent dies. LOVINGLY address defiant behavior.

Children will revisit grief at certain milestones

When there is a spousal death, remember that your family needs you.

Be sensitive to your family's needs. Be aware that you are not the only one hurting.

Make sure that you do not do all your grieving behind closed doors in secret. It's appropriate for your children to see you sad. In a healthy, healing family you must grieve openly because children learn from your behavior.

Be aware of the health of your family. Make sure everyone is getting enough rest and eating more than just junk food.

Make sure everyone knows it is ok, to talk about the loss the family suffered. It's ok to talk about the one that died. It will help the remaining family unit to heal.

Am I Ever Going to Get Better, or Am I Stuck in Grief? And More Things to Remember on This Journey

Death rocks us to our core, so there are reasons why we must be intentional about our healing.

Bad days are normal.

It's okay. Call it a day, and start again tomorrow.

It becomes a problem when we just linger there.

God's Word declares that "We walk THROUGH the valley of the shadow of death" (Psalms 23). That is the key- we walk through the valley. We do not build a house there and move in.

Has my grieving gone on too long?

We must figure out how long "too long" is. And might I add, not to other people's standards or timelines? Remember, grief can be very self-focused when it happens to us, but there is a time when we must move forward. It takes work on our part to move on.

We need trusted friends, advisors, or counselors to help us realize if we are "stuck."

To figure out what too long is, you need to ask yourself, "Am I moving forward, am I beginning to grow?"

To grow into the person that this new journey has brought us, we must decide "I don't want to be here always, **I WANT** to heal." It takes little choices to move on with life, but some people are unwilling to make any forward-moving choices.

Again, a personal reference.

A few years ago, I had an accident at work that resulted in a substantial injury to my arm. The injury required immediate surgery to repair the damage. Over a process of time, the injury has healed. Not because I willed it to, not because I wanted it to be better, and not because I wanted things to be the same as they used to be. It healed because God designed our bodies to heal. He did not intend for us to go around with gaping wounds that would always be open and never heal. In the same way, God has designed our spirits to heal as well. It is God's will that we recover from our tragedies and losses and move into the fullness of life.

Yes, I will carry the scar that resulted from that incident for the rest of my life. It is a reminder to me of what I went through, but it is no longer the open painful wound that it was at first.

People often say "Time heals all wounds." Time does **not** heal all wounds, but it is a great buffer.

Wounds often leave scars.

No one grieves perfectly. It's easy to get caught up in grief when we don't move along in the healing process.

Grief reveals many things about us, and one of them is how we **really** feel about God and His goodness. It can also reveal anger, bitterness, and doubt. Lies are at the root of anger and bitterness after loss. "Someone has been taken from me that I can't live without. There is no way out of what I am experiencing, I am trapped. I cannot do this. My life is over." We must monitor our thoughts and our feelings. Thoughts affect our behavior and our behavior affects our feelings, and our feelings affect our actions. What starts as just thinking you want to roll over and forget it, turns into staying in bed all day staring endlessly at the TV. These actions contribute to staying stuck in grief.

It is hard to say, and even harder to accept. People make choices to stay in the throes of grief.

What a person sows, will also be what is reaped. (Galatians 6:7). If I am lonely, am I not connecting with my friends?

Do I ignore texts, emails, or phone calls from the people in my life who care for me?

Am I pushing away my friends and family with anger or bitterness? Do I make everyone walk on eggshells around me?

Am I constantly maximizing my loss and minimizing my blessings?

Grief is not just something to survive. It can teach us so much.

Remember, our loss does not define us. I am a widow, but I am also a productive person. I lost my child, but I am also a teacher. I am a widower, but I also work hard to provide for my family.

HERE ARE A FEW MORE THINGS TO REMEMBER ALONG OUR JOURNEY

Death puts things into perspective. It teaches us a lot about life.

After death, we become more selective about what we value.

How could a high electric bill scare me now? I've faced worse than that.

What does it matter if those shoes I wanted will NOT go on sale? Is my child's "D" on a test worth a heated argument?

> *Death makes us understand what really matters are people, not things.*

Trying to describe what you are feeling when you are grieving...the sadness, the loneliness, the emptiness, the confusion, is just as impossible as describing the chocolate milkshake, that we talked about in the Key Takeaways in the Introduction.

Death transforms us...we are not the person we used to be. And we will never actually be that person again. That being said, we do not have to go around like Eeyore, thinking the worst of every situation.

In walking alongside someone on their grief journey, we have learned that hurting people, hurt people. Sometimes people hurt so badly that they don't always guard what they say to other people. Things like:

"You could never understand" or "You have no idea what I am going through" While that is true, it's unfair to make people uncomfortable. When in the throes of grief, don't use others as a lightning rod for your own anger and frustration.

Try to understand grieving people are in a dark place right now, give them a measure of grace, and forgive them.

We have learned that often grieving people have to deal with poor comforters. People do mean well, they just don't know what to say, so often they say things that hurt us, make us mad, or are just plain ridiculous. Release things that people have said in error. Sometimes people will say something that is a quick fix, not understanding your pain or your situation. Things like, "I understand how you feel," when in reality, they cannot understand, because they don't know your relationship with the person that died.

We can make some people uncomfortable with our loss because people so often don't understand the depth of who we have lost. We think when it is **our** suffering, we can only marvel at the fact that the world did not stop and take notice of what you have lost. But in truth, others have had a loss in their own lives. We need to remember we are not the only ones to suffer loss.

People WILL forget dates that are important to us. Again forgive them and know that this is YOUR journey.

Again, this is just a manual to assist YOU while you are helping others walk their Journey Through Grief. No doubt you have your own experiences to draw from. God bless you in this ministry.

Key Takeaways

Bad days are normal.

Has my grieving gone on too long?

People often say "Time heals all wounds."

No one grieves perfectly.

Grief reveals many things about us

Grief is not just something to survive....It can teach us so much. Death puts things into perspective. It teaches us a lot about life. Death makes us understand what really matters are people, not things. Death transforms us.....we are not the person we used to be.

Hurting people, hurt people.

We need to remember we are not the only ones who have suffered loss.

www.ingramcontent.com/pod-product-compliance
Lightning Source LLC
Chambersburg PA
CBHW081725120626
46550CB00010B/3262